Classical Themes

Favorite orchestral works arranged for piano solo
by Fred Kern, Phillip Keveren, and Mona Rejino

Text Author
Barbara Kreader

Editor
Margaret Otwell

D0613698

Classical Themes Level 2 is designed for use with the second book of any piano method. Some methods may label their second book as *Book 2* (such as the *Hal Leonard Student Piano Library*), and others may label their second book as *Book 1*.

Concepts in *Classical Themes Level 2*:

Range	Symbols
(notation)	p, f, mp, mf, ♯, ♭, ♮, rit. ... D.S. al Fine 1. 2.

Rhythm	Intervals
4/4 time signature, 3/4 time signature	2nd, 3rd, 4th and 5th melodic and harmonic

To access audio visit:
www.halleonard.com/mylibrary

Enter Code
2866-7385-7345-8227

ISBN 978-1-4950-4762-6

HAL•LEONARD®
CORPORATION

7777 W. BLUEMOUND RD. P.O.BOX 13819 MILWAUKEE, WI 53213

In Australia Contact:
Hal Leonard Australia Pty. Ltd.
4 Lentara Court
Cheltenham, Victoria, 3192 Australia
Email: ausadmin@halleonard.com.au

Visit Hal Leonard Online at
www.halleonard.com

Table of Contents

About the Compositions

Symphony No. 9 "From The New World" (Largo) 6
Antonín Dvorák (1841-1904)

The Czech composer Antonín Dvorák liked to use folk melodies from his native country in nearly all of his compositions. At one point in his career, Dvorák came to the United States to direct the newly formed New York Conservatory. Extremely homesick during that time, he composed his *Symphony From The New World,* combining the Slavic color and character of the music of the Czech people with new musical influences he experienced in the United States. The theme of the symphony's slow movement expresses Dvorák's longing for his homeland.

March Militaire, Opus 51, No. 1 8
Franz Schubert (1797-1828)

The Viennese composer Franz Schubert is renowned for his outstandingly beautiful vocal melodies. He wrote over 600 songs in his short lifetime! Schubert often composed vibrant piano accompaniments to help characterize and give color to his melodies. In *March Militaire,* the rhythm defines the melodic interest and calls up images of soldiers marching. This charming piece was originally a duet for one-piano, four hands, and was the first of a set of three military marches, Opus 51.

Symphony No. 94 "Surprise" 10
Franz Joseph Haydn (1732-1809)

The Austrian composer Franz Josef Haydn, often known as the "Father of the Symphony," composed 104 symphonies. According to legend, Haydn, a joyful and playful person by nature, wanted to add something to his 94th symphony that would make listeners sit up and take notice. So he added a "surprise" during the slow, quiet second movement – a crashing chord that sounds on a weak beat.

Plaisir d'amour "The Joy Of Love" 12
Johann Paul (Jean-Paul) Martini (1741-1816)

The German/French composer Johann Paul (Jean-Paul) Martini was a successful court musician who wrote songs, operas, theater, chamber and band music. He also taught at the Paris Conservatoire and wrote several books about theory and music education. His sad and sentimental song *Plaisir d'amour (The Pleasures of Love)* is from his first collection of songs. In his time, Martini's varied songs with their pastoral, narrative, romantic and comic moods, were models for all other composers.

In The Hall Of The Mountain King from PEER GYNT.....................................14
Edvard Grieg (1843-1907)

The Norwegian composer Edvard Grieg loved to write short pieces that tell a story, and playwrights often asked him to create music for their dramas. *In the Hall of the Mountain King* appears in Act II of his countryman Henrik Ibsen's play *Peer Gynt.* The wild daughters of the king dance to this grotesque ballet music as they tease Peer because he is in love with one of them.

Alleluia from the motet EXSULTATE, JUBILATE
Wolfgang Amadeus Mozart (1756-1791)

The Austrian composer Wolfgang Amadeus Mozart began writing music at age five. When he was six, his father, Leopold, began taking Wolfgang and his sister, Nannerl, on tour to the castles of Europe's nobility. The young musicians would spend their days traveling in drafty, bumpy coaches and their evenings all dressed up, waiting around for the nobility to finish their elaborate dinners. Then, late at night, Wolfgang and Nannerl would be forced to show off their electrifying talents. Mozart's music is sublime, expressing a depth of emotion that is unparalleled in music history. He wrote the motet *Exsultate, Jubilate (Rejoice, Be Glad)* for soprano, organ and orchestra. The third part is the famous *Alleluia,* a joyful song of praise.

Barcarolle from the opera THE TALES OF HOFFMANN
Jacques Offenbach (1819-1880)

People most remember the German/French composer Jacques Offenbach as a man who liked to make people laugh. His music for such productions as *Orpheus In The Underworld* poked fun at people and at life. Yet Offenbach longed to be accepted as a serious composer. He hoped his opera *The Tales of Hoffmann* would bring him that recognition. During the opera, Hoffmann tells the story of his three loves: Olympia the doll, Antonia the singer, and Giulietta the beautiful maid. The beautiful *Barcarolle* is sung by Giulietta and Hoffmann's friend Nicklausse as they ride a gondola on the canals of Venice.

Romanze from EINE KLEINE NACHTMUSIK "A Little Night Music"
Wolfgang Amadeus Mozart (1756-1791)

Wolfgang Amadeus Mozart's *Eine Kleine Nachtmusik (A Little Night Music)* is perhaps his most popular work for chamber ensemble. The music is simple and entertaining, yet Mozart wrote it with the greatest artistic skill and musical understanding. The *Romanze* is one of five original movements in this chamber work for two violins, viola, cello, and solo bass. During the Baroque and Classical periods, chamber works were performed in small rooms (chambers or salons) for an invited audience, rather than in large concert halls.

Hallelujah from the oratorio MESSIAH
George Frideric Handel (1685-1759)

The German composer George Frideric Handel loved to travel, especially to Italy. There he fell in love with Italian melodies, which strongly influenced his compositional style. Handel eventually settled in England, where he wrote many oratorios – musical dramas for vocal soloists, chorus and orchestra designed to be performed without scenery, costumes or action – based on religious themes. His *Messiah* focuses on the life of Christ. The melodies in this work have such beautiful regular phrases that, at the time of its first performance, legend has it that one singer wrote in her score "I love Handel." We still do today. The sound of the *Hallelujah* chorus rings out from symphony halls and churches every year at Christmas and Easter time.

Waltz from the ballet THE SLEEPING BEAUTY
Pyotr Il'yich Tchaikovsky (1840-1893)

During the time the French dancer and choreographer Marius Petipa directed the Russian Imperial Ballet, he produced forty-six original ballets. When he decided to create a ballet based on Perrault's fairy tale *Sleeping Beauty*, he asked Pyotr Il'yich Tchaikovsky to write the music. The Russian composer's soaring orchestral sounds set the stage for this magical story. After the Prince rescues Sleeping Beauty from the witch's curse, he takes her into his arms and they waltz to this sweeping, powerful music.

Symphony No. 9
"From The New World"
Second Movement Theme (Largo)

Antonín Dvořák (1841 - 1904)
Czech Republic
Originally for orchestra
Arranged by Mona Rejino

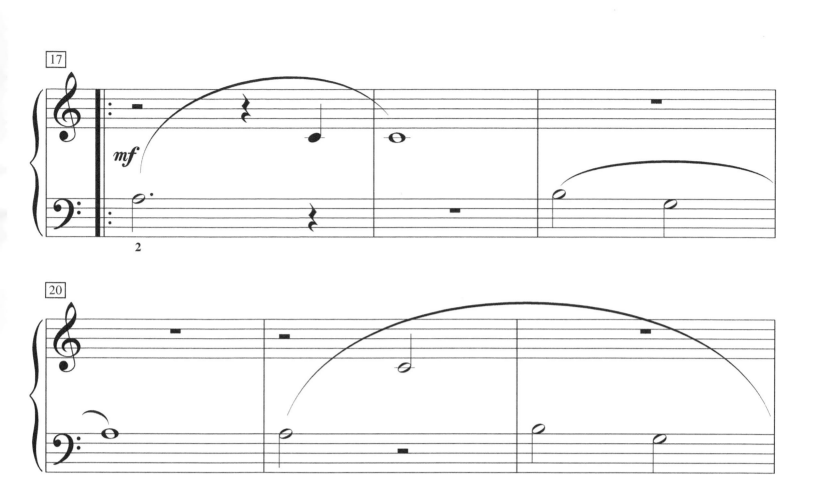

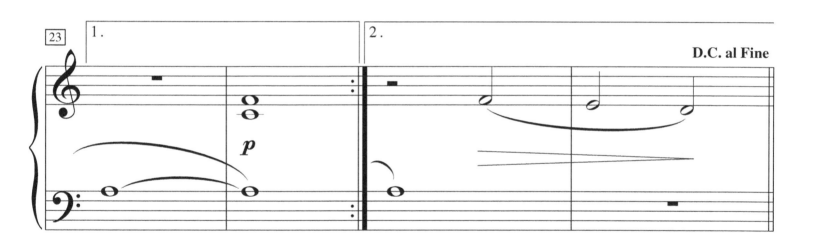

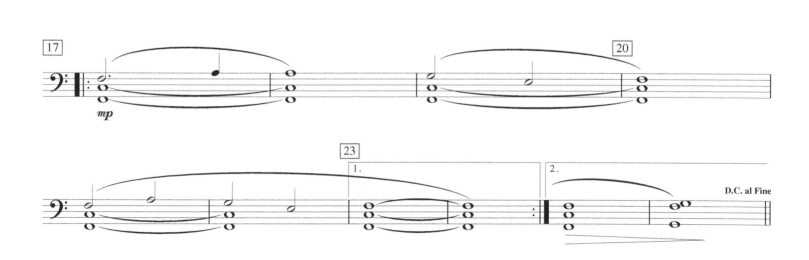

March Militaire
Opus 51, No. 1

Franz Schubert (1797 - 1828)
Austria
Originally for piano duet;
later arranged for orchestra
Arranged by Fred Kern

Allegro (♩ = 144)

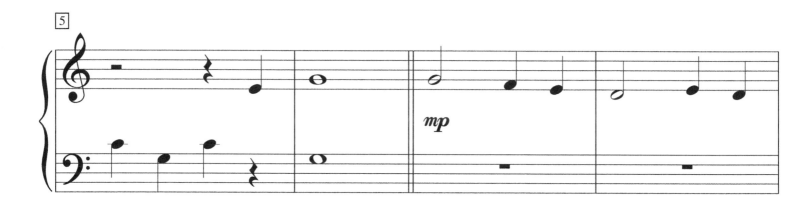

Accompaniment (Student plays one octave higher than written.)

Allegro (♩ = 144)

Symphony No. 94

"Surprise"
Second Movement Theme

Franz Joseph Haydn (1732 - 1809)
Austria
Originally for orchestra
Arranged by Fred Kern

Accompaniment (Student plays one octave higher than written.)

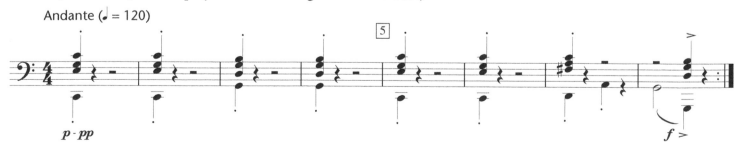

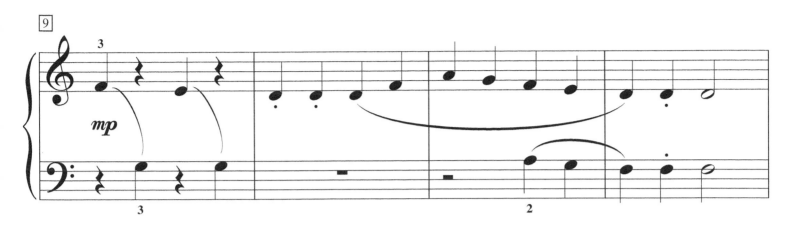

Plaisir d'amour
"The Joy Of Love"

Johann Paul (Jean-Paul) Martini (1741 - 1816)
Germany/France
Originally for voice and keyboard
Arranged by Fred Kern

Accompaniment (Student plays one octave higher than written.)

In The Hall Of The Mountain King

from PEER GYNT

Edvard Grieg (1843 - 1907)
Norway
Originally for orchestra
Arranged by Phillip Keveren

Accompaniment (Student plays one octave higher than written.)

Alleluia
from the motet EXSULTATE, JUBILATE

Wolfgang Amadeus Mozart (1756 - 1791)
Austria
Originally for soprano and orchestra
Arranged by Mona Rejino

Allegro, in 'two' (♩ = 92)

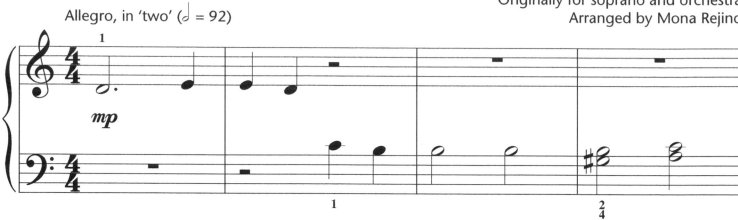

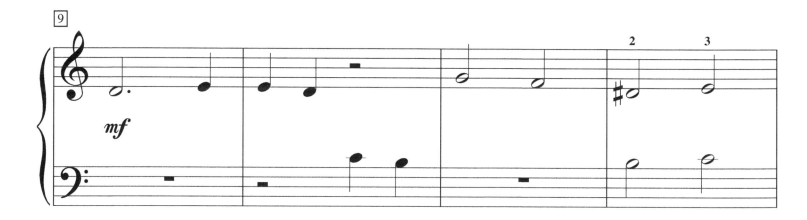

Accompaniment (Student plays one octave higher than written.)

Allegro, in 'two' (♩ = 92)

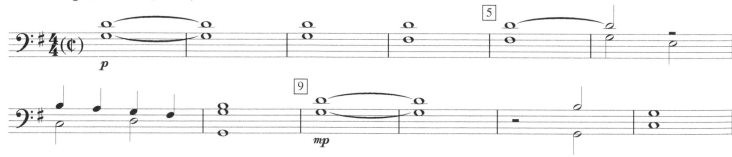

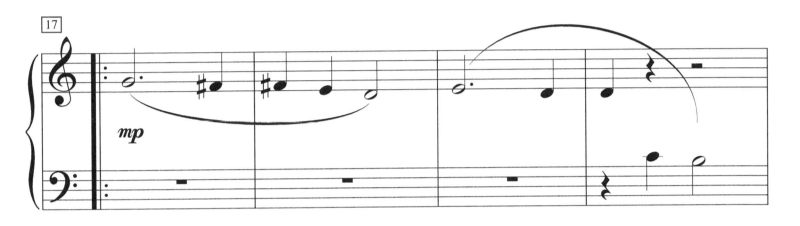

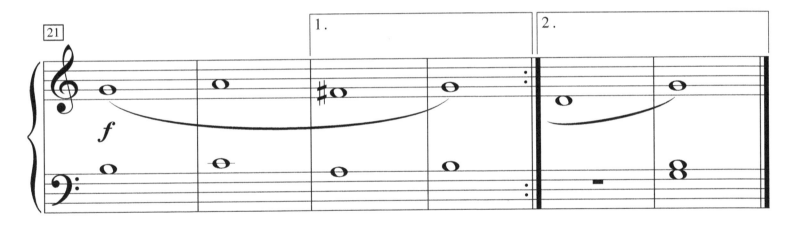

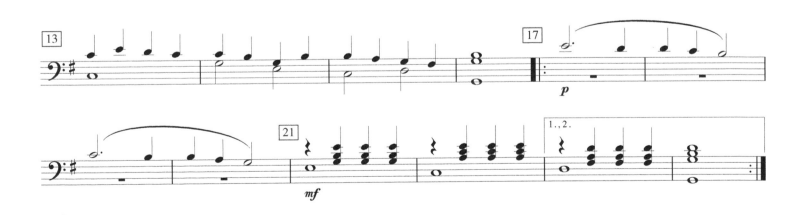

Barcarolle

from the opera LES CONTES D'HOFFMANN
(The Tales Of Hoffmann)

Jacques Offenbach (1819 - 1880)
France
Originally for vocal duet and orchestra
Arranged by Phillip Keveren

Accompaniment (Student plays one octave higher than written.)

Romanze

from EINE KLEINE NACHTMUSIK
"A Little Night Music"
Second Movement Theme

Wolfgang Amadeus Mozart (1756 - 1791)
Austria
Originally for string ensemble
Arranged by Phillip Keveren

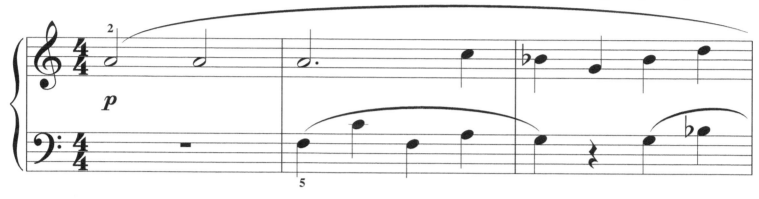

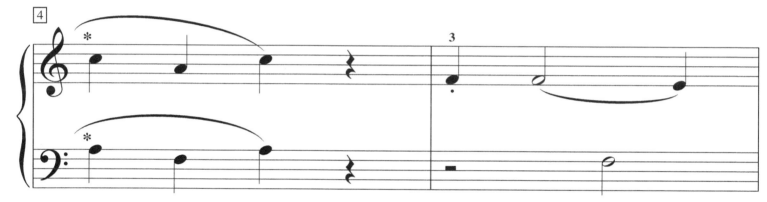

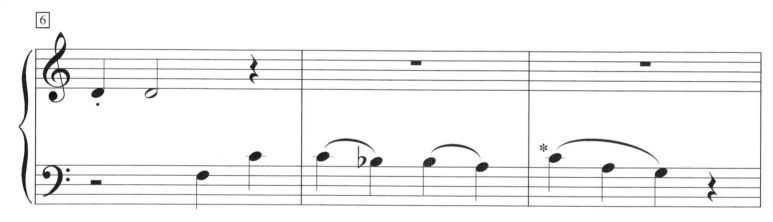

* = student may play ♩ ♪♪ 𝄽

Accompaniment (Student plays one octave higher than written.)

Hallelujah

from MESSIAH

George Frideric Handel (1685 - 1759)
Germany/England
Originally for chorus and orchestra
Arranged by Mona Rejino

Allegro, in 'two' (♩ = 76)

Accompaniment (Student plays one octave higher than written.)

Allegro, in 'two' (♩ = 76)

Waltz
from the ballet THE SLEEPING BEAUTY

Pyotr Il'yich Tchaikovsky (1840 - 1893)
Russia
Originally for orchestra
Arranged by Phillip Keveren

Accompaniment (Student plays one octave higher than written.)

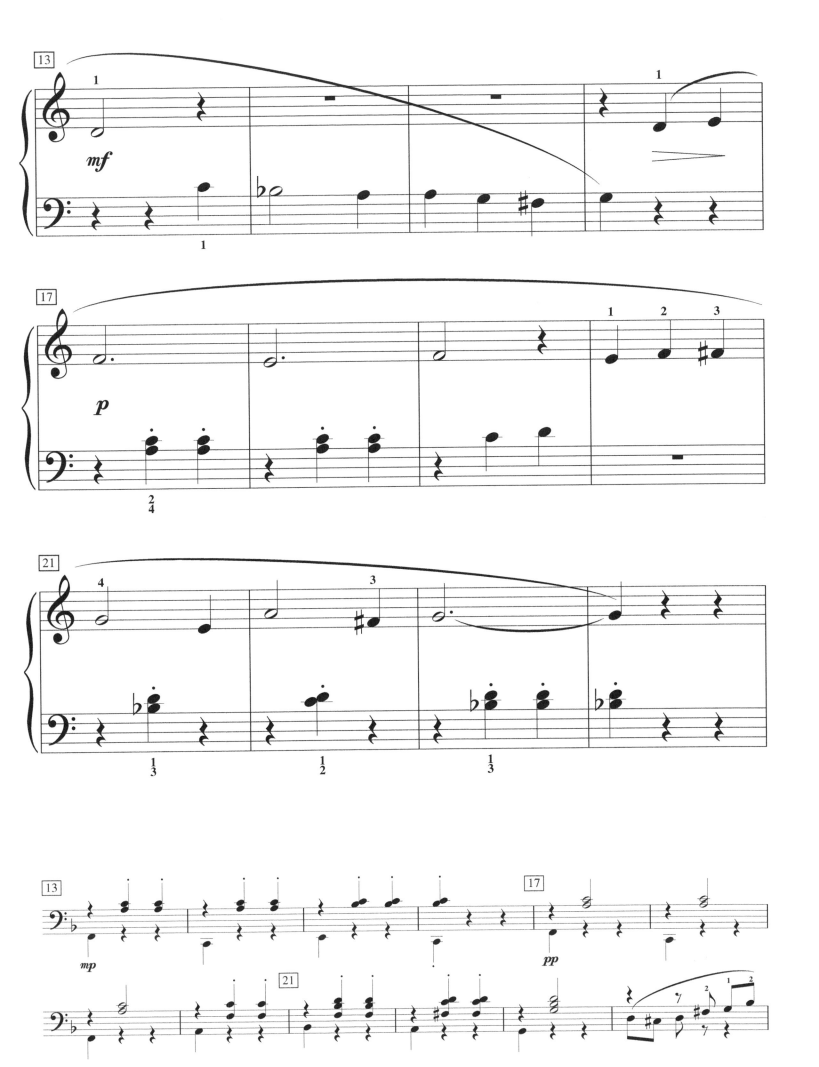

* Measures 25-30 can be counted as a series of half notes (1-2,1-2)

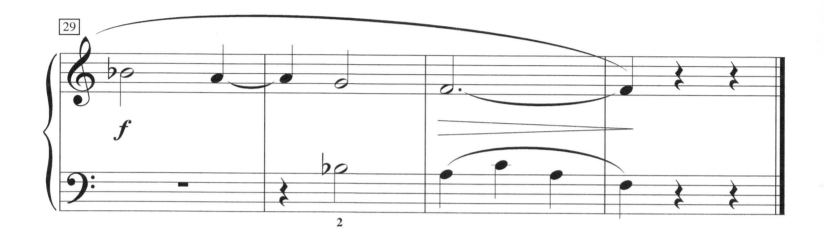

THE MIDDLE AGES

400 AD	600	800	1000	1200	1400

MUSIC

During the Middle Ages (also called the *Medieval Period*), the Roman Catholic church was the most powerful influence in European life. The church's music was a collection of ancient melodies called *plainsong* or *chant*, sung in unison (single line) with Latin words. The chants were organized in about 600 AD by Pope Gregory, and these official versions are known as *Gregorian chant*. Later, simple harmonies were added, and eventually the harmony parts became independent melodies sung with the main tune. This is called *polyphony*. Church music was written down using *neumes*, or square notes.

Outside the churches, traveling entertainers called *troubadours* or *minstrels* would sing songs about life and love in the language of the scommon people. This music was more lively and would often be accompanied by a drum, a wooden flute or an early form of the guitar called a *lute*.

• Plainsong   • Gregorian Chant   • Harmony   • Polyphony
• Troubadours

400 AD	600	800	1000	1200	1400

ART & LITERATURE

• Dante, author
(*The Divine Comedy*)

• Romanesque architecture   • Chaucer, author
(*Canterbury Tales*)

• Gothic architecture   • Donatello, artist (*David*)

400 AD	600	800	1000	1200	1400

WORLD EVENTS

• Fall of Roman Empire (*476 AD*)   • Charlemagne, Holy Roman Emperor   • First Crusade begins (*1096*)   • The Black Death
(*bubonic plague*)

• Rise of European universities

• Muhammad, prophet of Islam faith   • The Magna Carta (*1215*)

• Hindu-Arabic numbers developed

• Gunpowder, compass, paper invented (*China*)   • Genghis Kahn rules Asia

• Marco Polo travels to China

• Mayan civilization   • Incan and Aztec civilizations

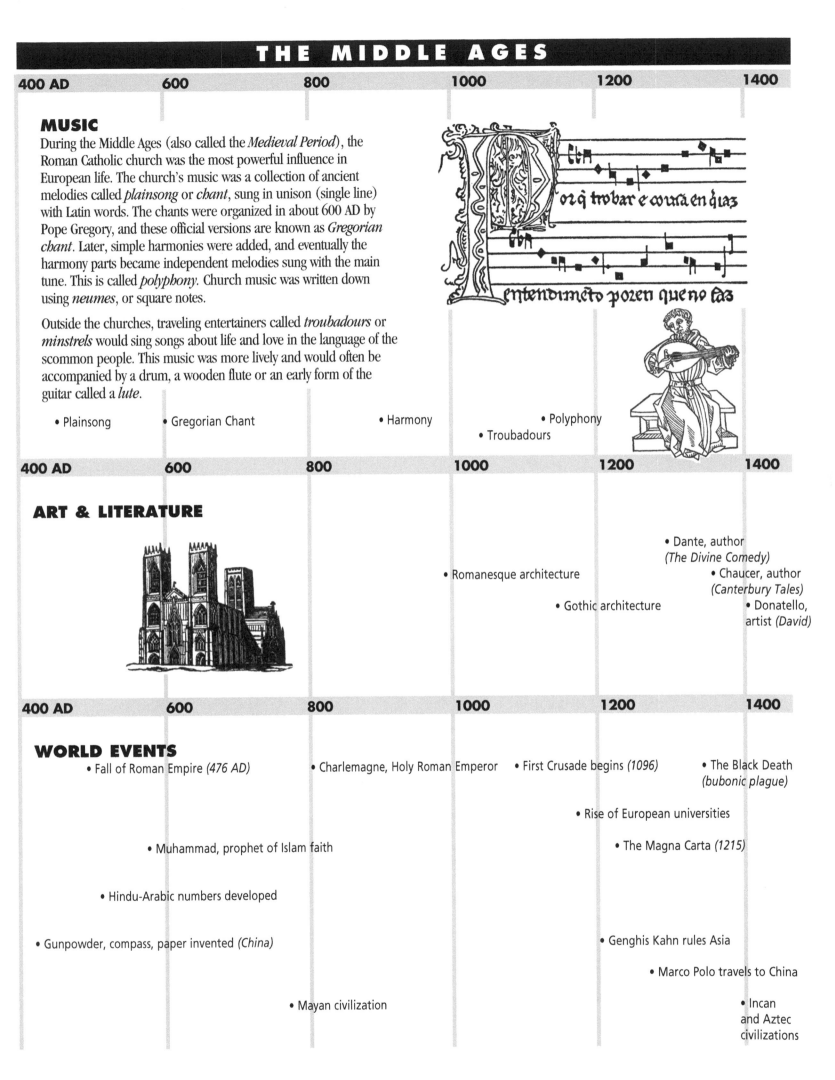

1450	1500	1550	1600

MUSIC

The era from about 1450–1600 was called the *Renaissance* ("rebirth") because people wanted to recreate the artistic and scientific glories of ancient Greece and Rome. It was also a time of discovery. The new printing press brought music to the homes of the growing middle class. European society became more *secular*, or non-religious, and concerts were featured in the halls of the nobility. An entertaining form of secular songs was the *madrigal*, sung by 4 or 5 voices at many special occasions. Instrumental music became popular, as new string, brass and woodwind instruments were developed.

A form of church music was the *motet*, with 3 or 4 independent vocal parts. In the new Protestant churches, the entire congregation sang *chorales*: simple melodies in even rhythms like the hymns we hear today. Important Renaissance composers were Josquin des Pres, Palestrina, Gabrielli, Monteverdi, William Byrd and Thomas Tallis.

• Protestant church music

• First printed music   • Madrigals

1450	1500	1550	1600

ART & LITERATURE

• Leonardo da Vinci, scientist/artist
(*Mona Lisa, The Last Supper*)

• Michelangelo, artist
(*Sistine Chapel, David*)

• Machiavelli,
author (*The Prince*)

• Shakespeare, author
(*Romeo and Juliet, Hamlet*)

1450	1500	1550	1600

WORLD EVENTS

• Gutenberg invents printing press *(1454)*   • Martin Luther ignites Protestant Reformation *(1517)*

• Columbus travels to America *(1492)*

• Magellan circles globe *(1519)*

• Copernicus begins modern astronomy *(1543)*

• First European contact with Japan *(1549)*

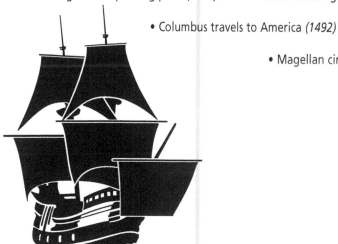

1600	1650	1700	1750

MUSIC

Music and the arts (and even clothing) became fancier and more dramatic in the *Baroque* era (about 1600-1750). Like the fancy decorations of Baroque church architecture, melodies were often played with *grace notes*, or quick nearby tones added to decorate them. Rhythms became more complex with time signatures, bar lines and faster-moving melodic lines. Our now familiar major and minor scales formed the basis for harmony, and chords were standardized to what we often hear today.

The harpsichord became the most popular keyboard instrument, with players often *improvising* (making up) their parts using the composer's chords and bass line. Violin making reached new heights in Italy. Operas, ballets and small orchestras were beginning to take shape, as composers specified the exact instruments, tempos and dynamics to be performed.

• Jean Baptiste Lully, French *(1632-1687)*

• Henry Purcell, English *(1658-1695)*

• Francois Couperin, French *(1668-1733)*

• Georg Philipp Telemann, German *(1681-1767)*

• Jean-Philippe Rameau, French *(1683-1764)*

• George Frideric Handel, German *(1685-1759)*

• Domenico Scarlatti, Italian *(1685-1757)*

J.S. Bach

1600	1650	1700	1750

ART & LITERATURE

• Cervantes, author *(Don Quixote)*

• Milton, author *(Paradise Lost)*

• Defoe, author *(Robinson Crusoe)*

• Rubens, artist *(Descent from the Cross)*

• Kabuki theater in Japan

• Rembrandt, artist *(The Night Watch)*

• Swift, author *(Gulliver's Travels)*

• Taj Mahal built *(1634-1653)*

1600	1650	1700	1750

WORLD EVENTS

• Salem witchcraft trials *(1692)*

• Galileo identifies gravity *(1602)*

• Louis XIV builds Versailles Palace *(1661-1708)*

• First English colony in America *(Jamestown, 1607)*

• Quebec founded by Champlain *(1608)*

• First slaves to America *(1619)*

• Isaac Newton *(1642-1727)* formulates principals of physics and math

1750	1775	1800	1820

MUSIC

The *Classical* era, from about 1750 to the early 1800's, was a time of great contrasts. While patriots fought for the rights of the common people in the American and French revolutions, composers were employed to entertain wealthy nobles and aristocrats. Music became simpler and more elegant, with melodies often flowing over accompaniment patterns in regular 4-bar phrases. Like the architecture of ancient *Classical* Greece, music was fit together in "building blocks" by balancing one phrase against another, or one entire section against another.

The piano replaced the harpsichord and became the most popular instrument for the *concerto* (solo) with orchestra accompaniment. The string quartet became the favorite form of *chamber* (small group) music, and orchestra concerts featured *symphonies* (longer compositions with 4 contrasting parts or *movements*). Toward the end of this era, Beethoven's changing musical style led the way toward the more emotional and personal expression of Romantic music.

Beethoven

Haydn

Mozart

- Franz Haydn, Austrian (German) *(1732-1809)*
- Johann Christian Bach, German *(1735-1782)*
- Muzio Clementi, Italian *(1752-1832)*
- Wolfgang Amadeus Mozart, German *(1756-1791)*

- Ludwig van Beethoven, German *(1770-1827)*
- Antonio Diabelli, Italian *(1781-1858)*
- Friedrich Kuhlau, German *(1786-1832)*

1750	1775	1800	1820

ART & LITERATURE

- Samuel Johnson, author *(Dictionary)*

   - Voltaire, author *(Candide)*

      - Gainsborough, artist *(The Blue Boy)*

      - *Encyclopedia Britannica*, first edition

- Wm. Wordsworth, author *(Lyrical Ballads)*

   - Goethe, author *(Faust)*

      - Goya, artist *(Witch's Sabbath)*

   - Jane Austen, author *(Pride and Prejudice)*

1750	1775	1800	1820

WORLD EVENTS

- Ben Franklin discovers electricity *(1751)*

   - American Revolution *(1775-1783)*

- French Revolution *(1789-1794)*

   - Napoleon crowned Emperor of France *(1804)*

   - Lewis and Clark explore northwest *(1804)*

      - Metronome invented *(1815)*

         - First steamship crosses Atlantic *(1819)*

THE ROMANTIC ERA

MUSIC

The last compositions of Beethoven were among the first of the new *Romantic* era, lasting from the early 1800's to about 1900. No longer employed by churches or nobles, composers became free from Classical restraints and expressed their personal emotions through their music. Instead of simple titles like *Concerto* or *Symphony*, they would often add descriptive titles like *Witches' Dance* or *To The New World*. Orchestras became larger, including nearly all the standard instruments we now use. Composers began to write much more difficult and complex music, featuring more "colorful" instrument combinations and harmonies.

Schumann

Nationalism was an important trend in this era. Composers used folk music and folk legends (especially in Russia, eastern Europe and Scandinavia) to identify their music with their native lands. Today's concert audiences still generally prefer the drama of Romantic music to any other kind.

Brahms

- Franz Schubert, German *(1797-1828)*
- Felix Mendelssohn, German *(1809-1847)*
- Friedrich Burgmuller, German *(1806-1874)*
- Frederic Francois Chopin, Polish *(1810-1849)*
- Robert Schumann, German *(1810-1856)*
- Franz Liszt, Hungarian *(1811-1886)*
- Stephen Heller, German *(1813-1888)*
- Fritz Spindler, German *(1817-1905)*

- Cornelius Gurlitt, German *(1820-1901)*
- Cesar Auguste Franck, French *(1822-1890)*
- Johannes Brahms, German *(1833-1897)*
- Camille Saint-Saens, French *(1835-1921)*
- Modest Mussorgsky, Russian *(1839-1881)*
- Peter Ilyich Tchaikovsky, Russian *(1840-1893)*
- Edvard Grieg, Norwegian *(1844-1908)*

ART & LITERATURE

- Charles Dickens, author *(The Pickwick Papers, David Copperfield)*

- Pierre Renoir, artist *(Luncheon of the Boating Party)*

- Harriet Beecher Stowe, author *(Uncle Tom's Cabin)*

- Lewis Carroll, author *(Alice In Wonderland)*

- Louisa May Alcott, author *(Little Women)*

- Jules Verne, author *(20,000 Leagues Under The Sea)*
- Claude Monet, artist *(Gare Saint-Lazare)*
- Mark Twain, author *(Tom Sawyer, Huckleberry Finn)*

- Vincent van Gogh, artist *(The Sunflowers)*
- Rudyard Kipling, author *(Jungle Book)*

WORLD EVENTS

- First railroad *(1830)*
- Samuel Morse invents telegraph *(1837)*
- First photography *(1838)*

- American Civil War *(1861-1865)*

- Alexander Graham Bell invents telephone *(1876)*

- Edison invents phonograph, practical light bulb, movie projector *(1877-1888)*

1900	1925	1950	1975	2000

- Edward MacDowell, American *(1861-1908)*
- Claude Debussy, French *(1862-1918)*
- Alexander Scriabin, Russian *(1872-1915)*
- Sergei Rachmaninoff, Russian *(1873-1943)*
- Arnold Schoenberg, German *(1874-1950)*
- Maurice Ravel, French *(1875-1937)*
- Bela Bartok, Hungarian *(1881-1945)*
- Heitor Villa-Lobos, Brazilian *(1881-1959)*
- Igor Stravinsky, Russian *(1882-1971)*
- Sergei Prokofieff, Russian *(1891-1952)*
- Paul Hindemith, German *(1895-1963)*
- George Gershwin, American *(1898-1937)*
- Aaron Copland, American *(1900-1990)*
- Aram Khachaturian, Russian *(1903-1978)*
- Dmitri Kabalevsky, Russian *(1904-1986)*
- Dmitri Shostakovich, Russian *(1906-1975)*
- Samuel Barber, American *(1910-1981)*
- Norman Dello Joio, American *(1913-   )*
- Vincent Persichetti, American *(1915-1987)*
- Philip Glass, American *(1937-   )*

MUSIC

The *20th century* was a diverse era of new ideas that "broke the rules" of traditional music. Styles of music moved in many different directions.

Impressionist composers Debussy and Ravel wrote music that seems more vague and blurred than the Romantics. New slightly-dissonant chords were used, and like Impressionist paintings, much of their music describes an impression of nature.

Composer Arnold Schoenberg devised a way to throw away all the old ideas of harmony by creating *12-tone* music. All 12 tones of the chromatic scale were used equally, with no single pitch forming a "key center."

Some of the music of Stravinsky and others was written in a *Neo-Classical* style (or "new" classical). This was a return to the Classical principals of balance and form, and to music that did *not* describe any scene or emotion.

Composers have experimented with many ideas: some music is based on the laws of chance, some is drawn on graph paper, some lets the performers decide when or what to play, and some is combined with electronic or other sounds.

Popular music like jazz, country, folk, and rock & roll has had a significant impact on 20th century life and has influenced great composers like Aaron Copland and Leonard Bernstein. And the new technology of computers and electronic instruments has had a major effect on the ways music is composed, performed and recorded.

1900	1925	1950	1975	2000

ART & LITERATURE

- Robert Frost, author *(Stopping by Woods on a Snowy Evening)*
- Pablo Picasso, artist *(Three Musicians)*
- J.R.R. Tolkien, author *(The Lord of the Rings)*
- F. Scott Fitzgerald, author *(The Great Gatsby)*
- Andy Warhol, artist *(Pop art)*
- Salvador Dali, artist *(Soft Watches)*
- Norman Mailer, author *(The Executioner's Song)*
- John Steinbeck, author *(The Grapes of Wrath)*
- Ernest Hemingway, author *(For Whom the Bell Tolls)*
- Andrew Wyeth, artist *(Christina's World)*
- George Orwell, author *(1984)*

1900	1925	1950	1975	2000

WORLD EVENTS

- First airplane flight *(1903)*
- Television invented *(1927)*
- Berlin Wall built *(1961)*
- Destruction of Berlin Wall *(1989)*
- World War I *(1914-1918)*
- World War II *(1939–1945)*
- John F. Kennedy assassinated *(1963)*
- First radio program *(1920)*
- Civil rights march in Alabama *(1965)*
- First satellite launched *(1957)*
- Man walks on the moon *(1969)*
- Vietnam War ends *(1975)*
- Personal computers *(1975)*

32